Great Americana

The Discoveries of John Lederer

John Lederer

The Discoveries
of John Lederer

by John Lederer

READEX MICROPRINT

Foreword

The Discoveries Of John Lederer, In three several Marches from Virginia, To the West of Carolina was translated from the Latin by Sir William Talbot and printed in London in 1672. Lederer provided the first written account of explorations to the Piedmont and to the Blue Ridge Mountains.

John Lederer, a German, came to Virginia for the purpose of finding a route across the Appalachian Mountains to the West. His first expedition, which he began in March, 1669, took him along the Pamunkey River to the Blue Ridge Mountains near what is today the site of Charlottesville, Virginia. He wandered some time in snow "hoping to finde some passage through the Mountains; but the coldness of the Air and Earth together, seizing my Hands and Feet with numbness, put me to a *ne plus ultra*," he said. On a second attempt in May-June, 1670, he arrived near the Catawba River. This time he halted his march because he "thought it not safe to venture my self amongst the Spaniards, lest taking me for a Spy, they would either make me away, or condemn me to a perpetual Slavery in their Mines." The third expedition which he set out upon in August of the same year reached the Shenandoah Valley near the present site of Front Royal, Virginia. However, wrote Lederer, "we unanimously agreed to return back, seeing no possibility of passing through the Mountains."

One of the reasons for Lederer's persistence in hunting for a passage across the mountains lay in his belief "that the Indian Ocean does stretch an Arm or Bay from California into the Continent as far as the Apalataean Mountains." Lederer expected others to continue what he had begun, and he offered advice based on his own experiences in the country. He suggested that future explorers march in parties "not...above half a dozen, or ten at the most...and of these, the major part Indians: for the Nations in your way are prone to jealousie and mischief towards Christians in a considerable Body, and as courteous and hearty to a few, from whom they apprehend no danger." Some of Lederer's most interesting comments have to do with the Indians he encountered. For all their lack of education and civilization, he respected their intelligence. After attending several of their meetings he said that "their Seniors deliver themselves with as much Judgement and Eloquence as I should have expected from men of Civil education and Literature."

Lederer later resided for a time in the colony of Maryland, where he received citizenship. But in 1675 he returned to his native Germany and apparently did not visit America again. The English translator of his *Discoveries*, Sir William Talbot, was secretary of the province of Maryland. Since Lederer's original Latin account has been lost, Talbot's translation is all that survived. Talbot dedicated the translation to Lord Ashley, later Earl of Shaftesbury. Lord Ashley was one of the most energetic supporters of colonization in Carolina. For additional information about Lederer see *The Discoveries of John Lederer*, ed. William P. Cumming (Charlottesville, 1958), pp. vii-x, 69-126.

The Discoveries of John Lederer

Licensed,

Nov. 1. 1671.

ROGER L'ESTRANGE.

THE
DISCOVERIES
OF
JOHN LEDERER,

In three feveral Marches from

VIRGINIA,

To the Weft of

Carolina,

And other parts of the Continent :

Begun in *March* 1669, and ended in *September* 1670.

Together with

A General MAP of the whole Territory
which he traverfed.

Collected and Tranflated out of Latine from his Difcourfe
and Writings,

By Sir *William Talbot* Baronet.

Sed nos immenfum fpatiis confecimus æquor,
Et jam tempus equum fumantia folvere colla.   Virg.Georg.

London, Printed by *J. C.* for *Samuel Heyrick,* at Grays-
Inne-gate in Holborn. 1672.

To the Right Honourable
ANTHONY Lord ASHLEY,
Baron Ashley of Wimborn St. Giles,
Chancellor of his Majesties Exchequer,
Under-Treasurer of England,
One of the Lords Commissioners of his Ma-
jesties Treasury, one of the Lords of his
most Honourable Privie Council,
and one of the Lords Proprie-
tors of CAROLINA.

MY LORD,

Rom this discourse it is clear
that the long looked-for
discovery of the *Indian* Sea
does nearly approach; and
Carolina, out of her happy
experience of your Lord-
ships success in great undertakings, presumes
that the accomplishment of this glorious
Designe is reserved for her. In order to
which, the *Apalataean* Mountains (though
like the prodigious Wall that divides *Chi-*

na

The Epistle Dedicatory

nia and *Tartary*, they deny *Virginia* passage
into the West Continent) stoop to your
Lordships Dominions, and lay open a Prospect into unlimited Empires ; Empires that
will hereafter be ambitious of subjection
to that noble Government which by your
Lordships deep wisdom and providence
first projected, is now established in *Carolina* ; for it will appear that she flourishes
more by the influence of that, than the advantages she derives from her Climate and
Soyl, which yet do render her the Beauty
and Envy of North-*America*. That all her
glories should be seen in this Draught, is
not reasonably to be expected, since she sate
to my Author but once, and then too with
a side-face; and therefore I must own it was
never by him designed for the Press, but
published by me, out of no other ambition
than that of manifesting to the world, that
I am

My Lord,
Your Lordships most humble
and obedient Servant,

William Talbot.

TO THE
READER.

Hat a Stranger *should presume* (though with Sir William Berkly's Commission) to go into those Parts of the American Continent where Englishmen never had been, and whither some refused to accompany him, was, in Virginia look'd on as so great an insolence, that our Traveller at his Return, instead of Welcom and Applause, met nothing but Affronts and Reproaches; for indeed it was their part, that forsook him in the Expedition, to procure him discredit that was a witness to theirs: Therefore no industry was wanting to prepare Men with a prejudice against him, and this their malice improved to such a general Animosity, that he was not safe in Virginia from the outrage of the People, drawn into a perswasion, that the Publick Levy of that year, went all to the ex-
pence

To the Reader.

pence of his Vagaries. Forced by this storm into Maryland, be became known to me, though then ill-affected to the Man, by the stories that went about of him: Nevertheless finding him, contrary to my expectation, a modest ingenious person, & a pretty Scholar, I thought it common Justice to give him an occasion of vindicating himself from what I had heard of him; which truly he did with so convincing Reason and circumstance, as quite abolished those former impressions in me, and made me desire this Account of his Travels, which here you have faithfully rendred out of Latine from his own Writings and Discourse, with an entire Map of the Territory he traversed, copied from his own hand. All these I have compared with Indian Relations of those parts (though I never met with any Indian that had followed a Southwest-Course so far as this German) and finding them agree, I thought the Printing of these Papers was no injury to the Author, and might prove a Service to the Publick.

William Talbot.

dom: Reg
Vshery
Wisacky
Sara
Watary
Shabocœnock
The R
Aken
Deserta arenosa
Tos ki ro

P a r s I n

Leagues
5 10 15 20

Cross Sculpsit

33   34   35

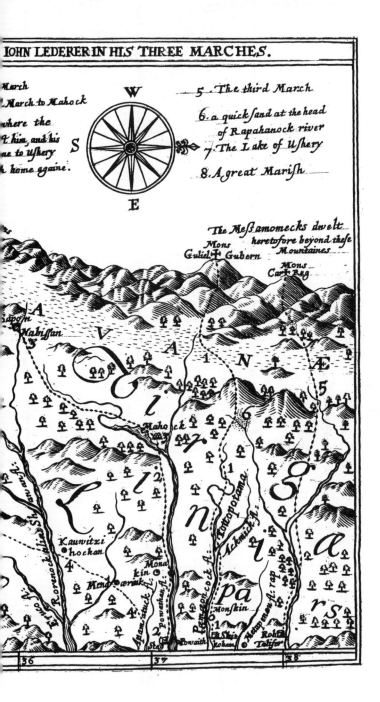

IOHN LEDERER IN HIS THREE MARCHES.

W

S

E

March
March to Mahock
where the
him, and his
ne to Ushery
home againe.

5. The third March

6. a quick sand at the head
   of Rapahanock river

7. The Lake of Ushery

8. A great Marish

The Meßamomecks dwelt
heretofore beyond these
Mountaines

Mons
Guliel Gubern

Mons
Cart Reg

A

V

Sapon
Nahissan
3

i

A

1

N

Æ

5

Mahock

6

7

1

L

l

2

n

Kontopotoma

g

a

Kauvitzi
hockan
4

i

Achmick fi

Mona
kin

Rappahanock fi:

Meng oerink

4

Attamuanock fi:

Powhatan fi:

pa
Monskin

2

r

s

Stegg Powaith

1

Ft. Skin
kohan

Matapment fi: rap

Robt
Talifer

36

37

38

THE

Discoveries of JOHN LEDERER
from *Virginia* to the West of *Carolina*,
and other parts of the Continent.

A General and brief Account of the North-American Continent.

Orth, as well as South-*America*, may be divided into three Regions : the Flats, the Highlands, and the Mountains. The Flats (in Indian, *Ahkynt*) is the Territory lying between the Eastern Coast, and the falls of the great Rivers , that there run into the *Atlantick* Ocean , in extent generally taken Ninety miles. The Highlands (in Indian , *Ahkontshuck*) begin at those falls, and determine at the foot of the great ridge of Mountains that runs thorow the midst of this Continent, Northeast and Southwest, called by the Spaniards *Apalatei*, from the Nation *Apalakin*; and by the Indians, *Pe-motinck*

motinck. According to the best of my observation and conjecture, they lie parallel to the *Atlantick* Sea-coast, that
bearing from *Canada* to Cape *Florida*, Northeast and Southwest, and then falling off due West as the Mountains do at
Sara : but here they take the name of *Suala* ; *Sara* in the
Warrennuncock dialect being *Safa* or *Sualy.*

The Flats, or *Abkynt*, are by former Writers made so well
known to Christendom, that I will not stop the Reader
here, with an unnecessary description of them ; but shall
onely say, that by the rankness of the Soyl, and salt moist-
ness of the Air, daily discoveries of Fish-shells three fathom
deep in the earth, and Indian tradition ; these parts are sup-
posed some Ages past to have lain under the Sea.

The Highlands (or *Abkontshuch*) though under the same
Parallels, are happie notwithstanding in a more temperate
and healthful Air. The ground is over-grown with under-
wood in many places, and that so perplext and interwoven
with Vines, that who travels here, must sometimes cut
through his way. These Thickets harbour all sorts of beasts
of prey, as Wolves, Panthers, Leopards, Lions, &c. (which
are neither so large nor so fierce as those of *Asia* and *Africa*)
and small Vermine, as wilde Cats, Foxes, Racoons. These
parts were formerly possessed by the *Tacci*, alias *Dogi* ; but
they are extinct ; and the Indians now seated here, are di-
stinguished into the several Nations of *Mahoe, Nuntaneuck,* a-
lias *Nuntaly, Nahyssan, Sapon, Managog, Mangoack, Akenatzy,* and *Monakin,* &c. One Language is common to them
all, though they differ in Dialects. The parts inhabited here
are pleasant and fruitful, because cleared of Wood, and laid
open to the Sun. The Valleys feed numerous herds of Deer
and Elks larger then Oxen : these Valleys they call *Savana,*
being Marish grounds at the foot of the *Apalatei,* and yearly laid und r water in the beginning of Summer by flouds
of melted Snow falling down from the Mountains.

The *Apalataan* Mountains, called in Indian *Pæmotinck,*
(or the origine of the Indians) are barren Rocks, and
there-

therefore deferted by all living creatures but Bears, who cave
in the hollow Cliffs. Yet do thefe Mountains fhoot out to
the Eaftward great Promontories of rich Land , known by
the high and fpreading trees which they bear : thefe Promontories, becaufe lower then the main Ridge, are called by
the Indians *Tanx--Pemotinck* (aliàs *Aquatt*). To the Northeaft the Mountains rife higher ; and at *Sara* they fink fo
low, that they are eafily paffed over : but here (as was faid
before) they change their courfe and name , running due
Weft, and being called *Snaly* : now the *Snalian* Mountains
rife higher and higher Weftward.

Of the Manners and Cuftoms of the Indians inhabiting the Weftern parts of Carolina and Virginia.

THe Indians now feated in thefe parts, are none of thofe
which the Englifh removed from *Virginia*, but a people driven by an Enemy from the Northweft, and invited to
fit down here by an Oracle above four hundred years fince,
as they pretend : for the ancient inhabitants of *Virginia*
were far more rude and barbarous , feeding onely upon raw
flefh and fifh, until thefe taught them to plant Corn , and
fhewed them the ufe of it.

But before I treat of their ancient Manners and Cuftoms,
it is neceffary I fhould fhew by what means the knowledge
of them hath been conveyed from former ages to pofterity.
Three ways they fupply their want of Letters : firft by
Counters, fecondly by Emblemes or Hieroglyphicks, third-
ly by Tradition delivered in long Tales from father to fon,
which being children they are made to learn by rote.

For

For Counters, they ufe either Pebbles, or fhort fcantlings of ftraw or reeds. Where a Battel has been fought, or a Colony feated, they raife a fmall Pyramid of thefe ftones, confifting of the number flain or tranfplanted. Their reeds and ftraws ferve them in Religious Ceremonies : for they lay them orderly in a Circle when they prepare for Devotion or Sacrifice ; and that performed, the Circle remains ftill ; for it is Sacriledge to difturb or to touch it : the difpofition and forting of the ftraws and reeds, fhew what kinde of Rites have there been celebrated, as Invocation, Sacrifice, Burial, &c.

The faculties of the minde and body they commonly exprefs by Emblems. By the figure of a Stag, they imply fwiftnefs ; by that of a Serpent, wrath ; of a Lion, courage ; of a Dog, fidelity : by a Swan, they fignifie the *Englifh*, alluding to their complexion, and flight over the Sea.

An account of Time, and other things, they keep on a ftring or leather-thong tied in knots of feveral colours. I took particular notice of fmall Wheels ferving for this purpofe amongft the *Oenocks*, becaufe I have heard that the *Mexicans* ufe the fame. Every Nation gives his particular Enfigne or Arms : The *Safquefahanaugh* a Tarapine, or fmall Tortoife ; the *Akenatzy's* a Serpent ; the *Nahyffanes* three Arrows, &c. In this they likewife agree with the *Mexican* Indians. *Vid. Jof. à Cofta.*

They worfhip one God, Creator of all things, whom fome call *Okeè*, others *Mannith* : to him alone the Highprieft, or *Periku*, offers Sacrifice ; and yet they believe he has no regard to fublunary affairs, but commits the Government of Mankinde to leffer Deities, as *Quiacofough* and *Tagkanyfough*, that is, good and evil Spirits : to thefe the inferiour Priefts pay their devotion and Sacrifice, at which they make recitals, to a lamentable Tune, of the great things done by their Anceftors.

From four women, *viz. Pafh, Sepoy, Askarin,* and *Marafkarin*, they derive the Race of Mankinde ; which they there-

therefore divide into four Tribes, diftinguifhed under thofe feveral names. They very religioufly obferve the degrees of Marriage, which they limit not to diftance of Kindred, but difference of Tribes, which are continued in the iffue of the Females: now for two of the fame Tribe to match, is abhorred as Inceft, and punifhed with great feverity.

Their places of Burial they divide into four quarters, affigning to every Tribe one: for, to mingle their bodies, even when dead, they hold wicked and ominous. They commonly wrap up the corpfe in beafts skins, and bury with it Provifion and Houfholdftuff for its ufe in the other world. When their great men die, they likewife flay prifoners of War to attend them. They believe the tranfmigration of fouls: for the Angry they fay is poffeft with the fpirit of a Serpent; the Bloudy, with that of a Wolf; the Timorous, of a Deer; the Faithful, of a Dog, &c. and therefore they are figured by thefe Emblemes.

Elizium, or the abode of their leffer Deities, they place beyond the Mountains and Indian Ocean.

Though they want thofe means of improving Humane Reafon; which the ufe of Letters affords us; let us not therefore conclude them wholly deftitute of Learning and Sciences: for by thefe little helps which they have found, many of them advance their natural underftandings to great knowledge in Phyfick, Rhetorick, and Policie of Government: for I have been prefent at feveral of their Confultations and Debates, and to my admiration have heard fome of their Seniors deliver themfelves with as much Judgement and Eloquence as I fhould have expected from men of Civil education and Literature.

The First EXPEDITION,

From the head of *Pemæoncock*, aliàs *York-River* (due West) to the top of the *Apalatæan* Mountains.

UPon the ninth of *March* 1669, (with three Indians whose names were *Magtakunh*, *Hopotthguoh*, and *Naunnugh*) I went out at the falls of *Pemæoncock*, aliàs *York-River* in *Virginia*, from an Indian Village called *Shickehamany*, and lay that night in the Woods, encountring nothing remarkable, but a Rattle-snake of an extraordinary length and thickness, for I judged it two yards and a half or better from head to tail, and as big about as a mans arm : by the distention of her belly, we believed her full with young ; but having killed and opened her, found there a small Squirrel whole ; which caused in me a double wonder : first, how a Reptile should catch so nimble a creature as a Squirrel ; and having caught it, how she could swallow it entire. The Indians in resolving my doubts, plunged me into a greater astonishment, when they told me that it was usual in these Serpents, when they lie basking in the Sun, to fetch down these Squirrels from the tops of trees, by fixing their eye stedfastly upon them ; the horrour of which strikes such an affrightment into the little-beast, that he has no power to hinder himself from tumbling down into the jaws of his enemy, who takes in all his sustenance without chewing, his teeth serving him onely to offend withal. But I rather believe what I have heard from others, that these Serpents climb the trees, and surprise their prey in the nest.

The next day falling into Marish grounds between *Pemæoncock* and the head of the River *Matapeneugh*, the heaviness of the way obliged me to cross *Pemæoncock*, where its North and

and South-branch (called *Ackmick*) joyn in one. In the Peninfula made by thefe two branches, a great Indian King called *Tottopottoma* was heretofore flain in Battel, fighting for the Chriftians againft the *Mahocks* and *Nahyffans*, from whence it retains his name to this day. Travelling thorow the Woods, a Doe feized by a wild Cat croffed our way; the miferable creature being even fpent and breathlefs with the burden and cruelty of her rider, who having faftned on her fhoulder, left not fucking out her bloud until fhe funk under him : which one of the Indians perceiving, let flie a luckie Arrow, which piercing him thorow the belly, made him quit his prey already flain, and turn with a terrible grimas at us; but his ftrength and fpirits failing him, we efcaped his revenge, which had certainly enfued, were not his wound mortal. This creature is fomething bigger then our Englifh Fox, of a reddifh grey colour, and in figure every way agreeing with an ordinary Cat; fierce, ravenous and cunning : for finding the Deer (upon which they delight moft to prey) too fwift for them, they watch upon branches of trees, and as they walk or feed under, jump down upon them. The Fur of the wilde Cat, though not very fine, is yet efteemed for its vertue in taking away cold Aches and Pains, being worn next to the body : their flefh, though rank as a Dogs, is eaten by the Indians.

The eleventh and twelfth, I found the ways very uneven, and cumbred with bufhes.

The thirteenth, I reached the firft Spring of *Pemæoncock*, having croffed the River four times that day, by reafon of its many windings ; but the water was fo fhallow, that it hardly wet my horfes pafterns. Here a little under the furface of the earth, I found flat pieces of petrified matter, of one fide folid Stone, but on the other fide Ifinglas, which I eafily peeled off in flakes about four inches fquare : feveral of thefe pieces, with a tranfparent Stone like Cryftal that cut Glafs, and a white Marchafite that I purchafed of the Indians, I prefented to Sir *William Berkley* Governour of *Virginia.*

The

The fourteenth of *March*, from the top of an eminent hill, I firft defcried the *Apalatean* Mountains, bearing due Weft to the place I ftood upon: their diftance from me was fo great, that I could hardly difcern whether they were Mountains or Clouds, until my Indian fellow-travellers proftrating themfelves in Adoration, howled out after a barbarous manner, *Okéepaze*, i. e. *God is nigh.*

The fifteenth of *March*, not far from this hill, paffing over the South-branch of *Rappahanock*-river, I was almoft fwallowed in a Quickfand. Great herds of Red and Fallow Deer I daily faw feeding; and on the hill-fides, Bears craffing Maft like Swine. Small Leopards I have feen in the Woods, but never any Lions, though their skins are much worn by the Indians. The Wolves in thefe parts are fo ravenous, that I often in the night feared my horfe would be devoured by them, they would gather up and howl fo clofe round about him, though Tether'd to the fame tree at whofe foot I my felf and the Indians lay : but the Fires which we made, I fuppofe, fcared them from worrying us all. Beaver and Otter I met with at every River that I paffed; and the Woods are full of Grey Foxes.

Thus I travelled all the fixteenth; and on the feventeenth of *March* I reached the *Apalatæi*. The Air here is very thick and chill; and the waters iffuing from the Mountainfides, of a Blue colour, and Allumifh tafte.

The eighteenth of *March*, after I had in vain affayed to ride up, I alighted, and left my horfe with one of the Indians, whilft with the other two I climbed up the Rocks, which were fo incumbred with bufhes and brambles, that the afcent proved very difficult : befides, the firft precipice was fo fteep, that if I lookt down, I was immediately taken with a fwimming in my head; though afterwards the way was more eafie. The height of this Mountain was very extraordinary : for notwithftanding I fet out with the firft appearance of light, it was late in the evening before I gained the top, from whence the next morning I had a beautiful pro-

prospect of the *Atlantick*-Ocean washing the *Virginian*-shore; but to the North and West, my sight was suddenly bounded by Mountains higher than that I stood upon. Here did I wander in Snow, for the most part, till the Four and twentieth day of *March*, hoping to finde some passage through the Mountains; but the coldness of the Air and Earth together, seizing my Hands and Feet with numbness, put me to a *ne plus ultra*; and therefore having found my *Indian* at the foot of the Mountain with my Horse, I returned back by the same way that I went.

The Second EXPEDITION,

From the Falls of *Powhatan*, aliàs *James-River*, in *Virginia*, to *Mahock* in the *Apalatæan* Mountains.

THe twentieth of *May* 1670, one Major *Harris* and my self, with twenty *Christian* Horse, and five *Indians*, marched from the Falls of *James-River*, in *Virginia*, towards the *Monakins*; and on the Two and twentieth were welcomed by them with Volleys of Shot. Near this Village we observed a Pyramid of stones piled up together, which their Priests told us, was the Number of an *Indian* Colony drawn out by Lot from a Neighbour-Countrey over-peopled, and led hither by one *Monack*, from whom they take the Name of *Monakin*. Here enquiring the way to the Mountains, an ancient Man described with a staffe two paths on the ground; one pointing to the *Mahocks*, and the other to the *Nahyssans*; but my *English* Companions slighting the *Indians* direction, shaped their course by the Compass due West, and therefore it fell out with us, as

C

it

it does with those Land-Crabs, that crawling backwards in a direct line, avoid not the Trees that stand in their way, but climbing over their very tops, come down again on the other side, and so after a days labour gain not above two foot of ground. Thus we obstinately pursuing a due West course, rode over steep and craggy Cliffs, which beat our Horses quite off the hoof. In these Mountains we wandred from the Twenty fifth of *May* till the Third of *June*, finding very little sustenance for Man or Horse; for these places are destitute both of Grain and Herbage.

The third of *June* we came to the South-branch of *James*-River, which Major *Harris* observing to run Northward, vainly imagined to be an Arm of the Lake of *Canada*; and was so transported with this Fancy, that he would have raised a Pillar to the Discovery, if the fear of the *Mahock Indian*, and want of food, had permitted him to stay. Here I moved to cross the River and march on; but the rest of the Company were so weary of the enterprize, that crying out, *One and All*, they had offered violence to me, had I not been provided with a private Commission from the Governour of *Virginia* to proceed, though the rest of the company should abandon me; the sight of which laid their fury.

The lesser Hills, or *Akontshuck*, are here unpassable, being both steep and craggy: the Rocks seemed to me at a distance to resemble Eggs set up an end.

James-River is here as broad as it is about an hundred mile lower at *Monakin*; the passage over is very dangerous, by reason of the rapid Torrents made by Rocks and Shelves forcing the water into narrow Chanels. From an observation which we made of straws and rotten chuncks hanging in the boughs of Trees on the Bank, and two and twenty foot above water, we argued that the melted Snow falling from the Mountains swelled the River to that height, the Flood carrying down that rubbish which, upon the abatement of the Inundation, remained in the Trees.

The

The Air in thefe parts was fo moift, that all our Bifcuit became mouldy and unfit to be eaten, fo that fome nicer ftomachs, who at our fetting out laughed at my provifion of *Indian*-meal parched, would gladly now have fhared with me: but I being determined to go upon further Difcoveries, refufed to part with any of that which was to be my moft neceffary fuftenance.

The Continuation of the Second Expedition from Mahock, Southward, into the Province of Carolina.

THe fifth of *June*, my Company and I parted good friends, they back again, and I with one *Safquefa-hanough-Indian*, named *Juckzetavon*, only, in purfuit of my firft Enterprize, changing my courfe from Weft to South-weft & by South, to avoid the Mountains. Major *Harris* at parting gave me a Gun, believing me a loft man, and given up as a prey to *Indians* or favage Beafts; which made him the bolder in *Virginia* to report ftrange things in his own praife and my difparagement, prefuming I would never appear to difprove him. This, I fuppofe, and no other, was the caufe that he did with fo much induftry procure me difcredit and odium; but I have loft nothing by it, but what I never ftudied to gain, which is Popular applaufe.

From the fifth, which was *Sunday*, until the ninth of *June*, I travelled through difficult Ways, without feeing any Town or *Indian*; and then I arrived at *Sapon*, a Village of the *Nahyffans*, about an hundred miles diftant from *Mahock*, fcituate upon a branch of *Shawan*, alias *Rorenock*-River; and though I had juft caufe to fear thefe *Indians*, becaufe they had been in continual Hoftility with the *Chriftians* for

ten years before ; yet prefuming that the Truck which I
carried with me would procure my welcome, I adventured
to put my felf into their power, having heard that they
never offer any injury to a few perfons from whom they apprehend no danger :   neverthelefs, they examined me ftrict-
ly whence I came, whither I went, and what my bufinefs
was. But after I had beftowed fome trifles of Glafs and
Metal amongft them, they were fatisfied with reafonable
anfwers, and I received with all imaginable demonftrations
of kindnefs, as offering of Sacrifice, a complement fhewed
only to fuch as they defign particularly to honour : but they
went further , and confulted their Godds whether they
fhould not admit me into their Nation and Councils, and
oblige me to ftay amongft them by a Marriage with the
Kings or fome of their great Mens Daughters. But I,
though with much a-do, waved their courtelie, and got my
Paffport, having given my word to return to them within
fix months.

Sapon is within the limits of the Province of Carolina,
and as you may perceive by the Figure, has all the attributes
requifite to a pleafant and advantagious Seat ; for though it
ftands high, and upon a dry land, it enjoyes the benefit of
a ftately River, and a rich Soyl, capable of producing many
Commodities, which may hereafter render the Trade of it
confiderable.

Not far diftant from hence, as I underftood from the
Nahyffan Indians, is their Kings Refidence, called Pintaha,
upon the fame River, and happy in the fame advantages
both for pleafure and profit : which my curiofity would
have led me to fee, were I not bound, both by Oath and
Commiffion, to a direct purfuance of my intended purpofe
of difcovering a paffage to the further fide of the Mountains.

This Nation is governed by an abfolute Monarch ; the
People of a high ftature, warlike and rich. I faw great ftore
of

of Pearl unbored in their little Temples, or Oratories, which they had won amongst other spoyls from the Indians of *Florida*, and hold in as great esteem as we do.

From hence, by the Indians instructions, I directed my course to *Akenatzy*, an Island bearing South & by West, and about fifty miles distant, upon a branch of the same River, from *Sapon*. The Countrey here, though high, is level, and for the most part a rich soyl, as I judged by the growth of the Trees; yet where it is inhabited by Indians, it lies open in spacious Plains, and is blessed with a very healthful Air, as appears by the age and vigour of the people; and though I travelled in the month of *June*, the heat of the weather hindred me not from Riding at all hours without any great annoyance from the Sun. By easie journeys I landed at *Akenatzy* upon the twelfth of *June*. The current of the River is here so strong, that my Horse had much difficulty to resist it; and I expected every step to be carried away with the stream.

This Island, though small, maintains many inhabitants, who are fix'd here in great security, being naturally fortified with Fastnesses of Mountains, and Water of every side. Upon the North-shore they yearly reap great crops of Corn, of which they always have a twelv-months Provision aforehand, against an Invasion from their powerful Neighbours. Their Government is under two Kings, one presiding in Arms, the other in Hunting and Husbandry. They hold all things, except their Wives, in common; and their custome in eating is, that every man in his turn feasts all the rest; and he that makes the entertainment, is seated betwixt the two Kings; where having highly commended his own chear, they carve and distribute it amongst the guests.

At my arrival here, I met four stranger-Indians, whose Bodies were painted in various colours with figures of Animals whose likeness I had never seen: and by some discourse and signes which passed between us, I gathered that they were the only survivours of fifty, who set out together

in

in company from fome great Ifland, as I conjecture, to the
Northweft ; for I underftood that they croffed a great Water, in which moft of their party perifhed by tempeft, the
reft dying in the Marifhes and Mountains by famine and
hard weather, after a two-months travel by Land and Water in queft of this Ifland of *Akenatzy.*

The moft reafonable conjecture that I can frame out of
this Relation, is, that thefe Indians might come from the
Ifland of new *Albion* or *California,* from whence we may
imagine fome great arm of the Indian Ocean or Bay ftretches
into the Continent towards the *Apalatæan* Mountains in the
nature of a mid-land Sea, in which many of thefe Indians
might have perifhed. To confirm my opinion in this point,
I have heard feveral Indians teftifie,that the Nation of *Rickohockans,* who dwell not far to the Weftward of the *Apalatæan* Mountains, are feated upon a Land, as they term it, of
great Waves ; by which I fuppofe they mean the Sea-fhore.

The next day after my arrival at *Akenatzy,*a *Rickohockan*
Ambaffadour, attended by five Indians, whofe faces were co-
loured with *Auripigmentum* (in which Mineral thefe parts
do much abound) was received, and that night invited
to a Ball of their fafhion ; but in the height of their mirth
and dancing, by a fmoke contrived for that purpofe, the
Room was fuddenly darkned, and for what caufe I know
not, the *Rickohockan* and his Retinue barbaroufly murthered.
This ftruck me with fuch an affrightment, that the very
next day, without taking my leave of them, I flunk away
with my Indian Companion. Though the defire of inform-
ing my felf further concerning fome Minerals, as *Auripigmentum, &c.* which I there took fpecial notice of, would
have perfwaded me to ftay longer amongft them, had not
the bloody example of their treachery to the *Rickohockans*
frighted me away.

The fourteenth of *June,*purfuing a South-fouthweft courfe,
fometimes by a beaten path , and fometimes over hills and
rocks,

rocks, I was forc'd to take up my quarters in the Woods : for though the *Oenock*-Indians, whom I then fought, were not in a direct line above thirty odde miles diftant from *A-kenatzy*, yet the Ways were fuch, and obliged me to go fo far about, that I reached not *Oenock* until the fixteenth. The Country here, by the induftry of thefe Indians, is very open, and clear of wood. Their Town is built round a field, where in their Sports they exercife with fo much labour and violence, and in fo great numbers, that I have feen the ground wet with the fweat that dropped from their bodies : their chief Recreation is Slinging of ftones. They are of mean ftature and courage, covetous and thievifh, induftrious to earn a peny ; and therefore hire themfelves out to their neighbours, who employ them as Carryers or Porters. They plant abundance of Grain, reap three Crops in a Summer, and out of their Granary fupply all the adjacent parts. Thefe and the Mountain-Indians build not their houfes of Bark, but of Watling and Plaifter. In Summer, the heat of the weather makes them chufe to lie abroad in the night under thin arbours of wilde Palm. Some houfes they have of Reed and Bark ; they build them generally round : to each houfe belongs a little hovel made like an oven, where they lay up their Corn and Maft, and keep it dry. They parch their Nuts and Acorns over the fire, to take away their rank Oylinefs ; which afterwards preff'd, yeeld a milky liquor, and the Acorns an Amber-colour'd Oyl. In thefe, mingled together, they dip their Cakes at great Entertainments, and fo ferve them up to their guefts as an extraordinary dainty. Their Government is Democratick ; and the Sentences of their old men are received as Laws, or rather Oracles, by them.

Fourteen miles Weft-Southweft of the *Oenocks*, dwell the *Shackory*-Indians, upon a rich Soyl, and yet abounding in Antimony, of which they fhewed me confiderable quantities. Finding them agree with the *Oenocks* in Cuftoms and Manners, I made no ftay here, but paffing thorow their

Town,

Town, I travelled till the nineteenth of *June*; and then
after a two days troubleſome Journey thorow Thickets and
Mariſh grounds, I arrived at *Watary* above fourty miles
diſtant, and bearing Weſt-Southweſt to *Shakor*. This Nation differs in Government from all the other Indians of theſe
parts : for they are Slaves,rather then Subjects to their King.
Their preſent Monarch is a grave man, and courteous to
ſtrangers : yet I could not without horrour behold his barbarous Superſtition, in hiring three youths, and ſending
them forth to kill as many young women of their Enemies
as they could light on, to ſerve his ſon, then newly dead, in
the other world, as he vainly fancyed. Theſe youths during
my ſtay returned with skins torn off the heads and faces of
three young girls, which they preſented to his Majeſtie, and
were by him gratefully received.

I departed from *Watary* the one and twentieth of *June*,
and keeping a Weſt-courſe for near thirty miles, I came to
Sara : here I found the ways more level and eaſie. *Sara* is
not far diſtant from the Mountains, which here loſe their
height, and change their courſe and name : for they run
due Weſt, and receive from the Spaniards the name of
Suala. From theſe Mountains or Hills the Indians draw
great quantities of *Cinabar*, with which beaten to powder
they colour their faces : this Mineral is of a deeper Purple
then *Vermilion*, and is the ſame which is in ſo much eſteem
amongſt Phyſitians, being the firſt element of Quickſilver.
I did likewiſe,to my no ſmall admiration,find hard cakes
of white Salt amongſt them : but whether they were made
of Sea-water, or taken out of Salt-pits, I know not : but
am apt to believe the later,becauſe the Sea is ſo remote from
them. Many other rich Commodities and Minerals there
are undoubtedly in theſe parts, which if poſſeſſed by an ingenious and induſtrious people, would be improved to vaſt
advantages by Trade. But having tied my ſelf up to things
onely that I have ſeen in my Travels, I will deliver no
Conjectures.   *Lin-*

Lingua file non est ultra narrabile quidquam.

Thefe Indians are fo indifcreetly fond of their children, that they will not chaftife them for any mifchief or infolence. A little Boy had fhot an Arrow thorow my body, had I not reconciled him to me with gifts : and all this anger was, becaufe I fpurred my horfe out of another Arrows way which he directed at him. This caufed fuch a mutiny amongft the Youth of the Town, that the Seniors taking my horfe and felf into protection, had much ado (and that by intreaties and prayers, not commands) to appeafe them.

From *Sara* I kept a South-Southweft courfe until the five and twentieth of *June*, and then I reached *Wifacky*. This three-days march was more troublefome to me then all my travels befides : for the direct way which I took from *Sara* to *Wifacky*, is over a continued Marifh over-grown with Reeds, from whofe roots fprung knotty ftumps as hard and fharp as Flint. I was forc'd to lead my horfe moft part of the way, and wonder that he was not either plunged in the Bogs, or lamed by thofe rugged knots.

This Nation is fubject to a neighbour-King refiding upon the bank of a great Lake called *Ufhery*, invironed of all fides with Mountains, and *Wifacky* Marifh ; and therefore I will detain the Reader no longer with the difcourfe of them, becaufe I comprehend them in that of *Ufhery*.

The fix and twentieth of *June*, having croffed a frefh River which runs into the Lake of *Ufhery*, I came to the Town, which was more populous then any I had feen before in my March. The King dwells fome three miles from it, and therefore I had no opportunity of feeing him the two nights which I ftayed there. This Prince, though his Dominions are large and populous, is in continual fear of the *Ouftack*-Indians feated on the oppofite fide of the Lake ; a people fo addicted to Arms, that even their women come into the field, and fhoot Arrows over their hufbands

D   bands

bands shoulders, who shield them with Leathern Targets. The men it seems should fight with Silver-Hatchets: for one of the *Usheryes* told me they were of the same metal with the Pomel of my Sword. They are a cruel generation, and prey upon people, whom they either steal, or force away from the *Usheryes* in *Periago*'s, to sacrifice to their Idols. The *Ushery*-women delight much in feather-ornaments, of which they have great variety; but Peacocks in most esteem, because rare in those parts. They are reasonably handsome, and have more of civility in their carriage then I observed in the other Nations with whom I conversed; which is the reason that the men are more effeminate and lazie.

These miserable wretches are strangely infatuated with illusions of the devil: it caused no small horrour in me, to see one of them wrythe his neck all on one side, foam at the mouth, stand bare-foot upon burning coals for near an hour, and then recovering his senses, leap out of the fire without hurt, or signe of any. This I was an eye-witness of.

The water of *Ushery*-lake seemed to my taste a little brackish; which I rather impute to some Mineral-waters which flow into it, then to any saltness it can take from the Sea, which we may reasonably suppose is a great way from it. Many pleasant Rivulets fall into it, and it is stored with great plenty of excellent fish. I judged it to be about ten leagues broad: for were not the other shore very high, it could not be discerned from *Ushery*. How far this Lake tends Westerly, or where it ends, I could neither learn or guess.

Here I made a days stay, to inform my self further in these Countries; and understood both from the *Usheries*, and some *Sara*-Indians that came to trade with them, that two-days journey and a half from hence to the Southwest, a powerful Nation of Bearded men were seated, which I suppose to be the Spaniards, because the Indians never have any; it being an universal custom amongst them, to prevent

their

their growth, by plucking the young hair out by the roots.
Weftward lies a Government inhofpitable to ftrangers; and
to the North, over the *Snala*-mountains, lay the *Rickohockans.* I thought it not fafe to venture my felf amongft the
Spaniards, left taking me for a Spy, they would either make
me away, or condemn me to a perpetual Slavery in their
Mines. Therefore not thinking fit to proceed further,
the eight and twentieth of *June* I faced about, and looked
homewards.

To avoid *Wifacky*-Marifh, I fhaped my courfe Northeaft;
and after three days travel over hilly ways, where I met
with no path or road, I fell into a barren Sandy defert,
where I fuffered miferably for want of water; the heat of
the Summer having drunk all the Springs dry, and left no
figne of any, but the Gravelly chanels in which they run:
fo that if now and then I had not found a ftanding Pool,
which provident Nature fet round with fhady Oaks, to defend it from the ardour of the Sun, my Indian companion,
horfe and felf had certainly perifhed with thirft. In this
diftrefs we travelled till the twelfth of *July*, and then found
the head of a River, which afterwards proved *Eruco*; in
which we received not onely the comfort of a neceffary and
feafonable refrefhment, but likewife the hopes of coming
into a Country again where we might finde Game for food
at leaft, if not difcover fome new Nation or People. Nor
did our hopes fail us: for after we had croffed the River
twice, we were led by it upon the fourteenth of *July* to the
Town of *Katearas*, a place of great Indian Trade and Com-
merce, and chief Seat of the haughty Emperour of the
Toskiroro's, called *Kaskufara*, vulgarly *Kaskous.* His grim
Majeftie, upon my firft appearance, demanded my Gun and
Shot; which I willingly parted with, to ranfom my felf
out of his clutches: for he was the moft proud imperious
Barbarian that I met with in all my Marches. The people
here at this time feemed prepared for fome extraordinary

Sole-

Solemnity : for the men and the women of better fort had
decked themfelves very fine with pieces of bright Copper in
their hair and ears, and about their arms and neck, which
upon Feftival occafions they ufe as an extraordinary brave-
ry :. by which it fhould feem this Country is not without
rich Mines of Copper. But I durft not ftay to inform my
felf further in it, being jealous of fome fudden mifchief towards me from *Kaskous*, his nature being bloudy, and pro-
voked upon any flight occafion.

Therefore leaving *Katearus*, I travelled through the
Woods until the fixteenth, upon which I came to *Ka-
witziokan*, an Indian town upon a branch of *Rorenoke*-ri-
ver, which here I paffed over, continuing my journey to
Menchœrinck ; and on the feventeenth departing from
thence, I lay all night in the Woods, and the next morning
betimes going by *Natoway*, I reached that evening *Apama-
tuck* in *Virginia*, where I was not a little overjoyed to fee
Chriftian faces again.

The third and laft EXPEDITION,

From the Falls of *Rappahanock*-River in *Virginia*, (due Weft) to the top of the *Apalatæan* Mountains.

ON the twentieth of *Auguft* 1670, Col. *Catlet* of *Virginia* and my felf, with nine Englifh Horfe, and five Indians on foot, departed from the houfe of one *Robert Talifer*, and that night reached the falls of *Rappahanock*-river, in
Indian *Mantepeuck*.

The next day we paffed it over where it divides into two
bran-

branches North and South, keeping the main branch North
of us.

The three and twentieth we found it so shallow, that it
onely wet our horses hoofs.

The four and twentieth we travelled thorow the *Savane*
amongst vast herds of Red and Fallow Deer which stood ga-
zing at us ; and a little after, we came to the Promontories
or Spurs of the *Apalatæan*-mountains.

These *Savanæ* are low grounds at the foot of the *Apalatæans*, which all the Winter, Spring, and part of the
Summer, lie under snow or water, when the snow is dissol-
ved, which falls down from the Mountains commonly a-
bout the beginning of *June* ; and then their verdure is
wonderful pleasant to the eye, especially of such as having
travelled through the shade of the vast Forest, come out of
a melancholy darknefs of a sudden, into a clear and open
skie. To heighten the beauty of these parts, the first
Springs of most of those great Rivers which run into the
Atlantick Ocean, or *Chefeapeack* Bay, do here break out, and
in various branches interlace the flowry Meads, whose luxu-
rious herbage invites numerous herds of Red Deer (for their
unusual largenefs improperly termed Elks by ignorant people) to feed. The right Elk, though very common in *New
Scotland, Canada,* and those Northern parts, is never seen on
this side of the Continent : for that which the *Virginians*
call Elks, does not at all differ from the Red Deer of *Europe,* but in his dimensions, which are far greater : but yet
the Elk in bignefs does as far exceed them : their heads, or
horns, are not very different ; but the neck of the Elk is so
short, that it hardly separates the head from the shoulders ;
which is the reason that they cannot feed upon level ground
but by falling on their knees, though their heads be a yard-
long : therefore they commonly either broufe upon trees, or
standing up to the belly in ponds or rivers feed upon the
banks : their Cingles or tails are hardly three inches long,
I have been told by a *New-England*-Gentleman , that the
lips

lips and noftrils of this creature is the moft delicious meat he ever tafted. As for the Red Deer we here treat of, I cannot difference the tafte of their flefh from thofe in *Europe*.

The fix and twentieth of *Auguft* we came to the Mountains, where finding no horfe-way up, we alighted, and left our horfes with two or three Indians below, whilft we went up afoot. The afcent was fo fteep, the cold fo intenfe, and we fo tired, that having with much ado gained the top of one of the higheft, we drank the Kings Health in Brandy, gave the Mountain His name, and agreed to return back again, having no encouragement from that profpect to proceed to a further difcovery; fince from hence we faw another Mountain, bearing North and by Weft to us, of a prodigious height: for according to an obfervation of the diftance taken by Col. *Catlet*, it could not be lefs then fifty leagues from the place we ftood upon.

Here was I ftung in my fleep by a Mountain-fpider; and had not an Indian fuckt out the poyfon, I had died: for receiving the hurt at the tip of one of my fingers, the venome fhot up immediately into my fhoulder, and fo inflamed my fide, that it is not poffible to exprefs my torment. The means ufed by my Phyfician, was firft a fmall dofe of Snake-root-powder, which I took in a little water; and then making a kinde of Plaifter of the fame, applied it neer to the part affected: when he had done fo, he fwallowed fome by way of Antidote himfelf, and fuckt my fingers end fo violently, that I felt the venome retire back from my fide into my fhoulder, and from thence down my arm: having thus fucked half a fcore times, and fpit as often, I was eafed of all my pain, and perfectly recovered. I thought I had been bit by a Rattle-fnake, for I faw not what hurt me: but the Indian found by the wound, and the effects of it, that it was given by a Spider, one of which he fhewed me the next day: it is not unlike our great blue Spider, onely it is fomewhat longer. I fuppofe the nature of his poyfon to be much like that of the *Tarantula*.

I

I being thus beyond my hopes and expectation restored to my self, we unanimously agreed to return back, seeing no possibility of passing through the Mountains: and finding our Indians with our horses in the place where we left them, we rode homewards without making any further Discovery.

CONJECTURES of the Land beyond the *Apalatæan* Mountains.

THey are certainly in a great errour, who imagine that the Continent of North-*America* is but eight or ten days journey over from the *Atlantick* to the *Indian* Ocean: which all reasonable men must acknowledge, if they consider that Sir *Francis Drake* kept a West-Northwest course from *Cape Mendocino* to *California*. Nevertheless, by what I gathered from the stranger Indians at *Akenatzy* of their Voyage by Sea to the very Mountains from a far distant Northwest Country, I am brought over to their opinion who think that the Indian Ocean does stretch an Arm or Bay from *California* into the Continent as far as the *Apalatæan* Mountains, answerable to the Gulfs of *Florida* and *Mexico* on this side. Yet I am far from believing with some, that such great and Navigable Rivers are to be found on the other side the *Apalatæans* falling into the Indian Ocean, as those which run from them to the Eastward. My first reason is derived from the knowledge and experience we already have of South-*America*, whose *Andes* send the greatest Rivers in the world (as the *Amazones* and *Rio de la Plata*, &c.) into the *Atlantick*, but none at all into the *Pacifique* Sea. Another Argument is, that all our Water-fowl which delight in Lakes and Rivers, as Swans, Geese,

Ducks,

Ducks, &c. come over the Mountains from the Lake of *Canada*, when it is frozen over every Winter, to our frefh Rivers ; which they would never do, could they finde any on the other fide of the *Apalatæans.*

INSTRUCTIONS to fuch as fhall march upon Difcoveries into the North-*American* Continent.

TWo breaches there are in the *Apalatæan* Mountains, o-pening a paffage into the Weftern parts of the Continent. One, as I am informed by Indians, at a place called *Zynodoa,* to the Norward ; the other at *Sara,* where I have been my felf : but the way thither being thorow a vaft Foreft, where you feldom fall into any Road or Path, you muft fhape your courfe by a Compafs ; though fome, for want of one, have taken their direction from the North-fide of the trees, which is diftinguifhed from the reft by quantities of thick Mofs growing there. You will not meet with many hinderances on horfeback in your paffage to the Mountains, but where your courfe is interrupted by branches of the great Rivers, which in many places are not Fordable ; and therefore if you be unprovided of means or ftrength to make a Bridge by felling trees acrofs, you may be forced to go a great way about : in this refpect company is neceffary, but in others fo inconvenient, that I would not advife a-bove half a dozen, or ten at the moft, to travel together ; and of thefe, the major part Indians : for the Nations in your way are prone to jealoufie and mifchief towards Chriftians in a confiderable Body, and as courteous and hearty to a few, from whom they apprehend no danger.

When you pafs thorow an even level Country, where
you

you can take no particular remarks from hill or waters to guide your felf by when you come back, you muft not forget to notch the trees as you go along with your fmall Hatchet, that in your return you may know when you fall into the fame way which you went. By this means you will be certain of the place you are in, and may govern your courfe homeward accordingly.

In ftead of Bread, I ufed the meal of parched *Mayz*, i. e. Indian Wheat ; which when I eat, I feafoned with a little Salt. This is both more portable and ftrengthning then Bifcuit, and will fuffer no mouldinefs by any weather. For other provifions, you may fecurely truft to your Gun, the Woods being full of Fallow, and *Savane* of Red-Deer ; befides great variety of excellent Fowl, as wilde Turkeys, Pigeons, Partridges, Phefants, &c. But you muft not forget to dry or barbecue fome of thefe before you come to the Mountains : for upon them you will meet with no Game, except a few Bears.

Such as cannot lie on the ground, muft be provided with light Hamacks, which hung in the trees, are more cool and pleafant then any bed whatfoever.

The Order and Difcipline to be obferved in this Expedition is, that an Indian Scout or two march as far before the reft of the company as they can in fight, both for the finding out provifion, and difcovery of Ambufhes, if any fhould be laid by Enemies. Let your other Indians keep on the right and left hand, armed not onely with Guns, but Bills and Hatchets, to build fmall Arbours or Cottages of boughs and bark of trees, to fhelter and defend you from the injuries of the weather. At nights it is neceffary to make great Fires round about the place where you take up your lodging, as well to fcare Wild-beafts away, as to purifie the air. Neither muft you fail to go the Round at the clofe of the evening : for then, and betimes in the morning, the Indians put all their defignes in execution : in the night they never attempt any thing.

F   When

When in the remote parts you draw near to an Indian Town, you muſt by your Scouts inform your ſelf whether they hold any correſpondence with the *Saſqueſabanaughs* : for to ſuch you muſt give notice of your approach by a Gun, which amongſt other Indians is to be avoided, becauſe being ignorant of their uſe, it would affright and diſpoſe them to ſome treacherous practice againſt you.

Being arrived at a Town, enter no houſe until you are invited ; and then ſeem not afraid to be led in pinion'd like a priſoner : for that is a Ceremony they uſe to friends and enemies without diſtinction.

You muſt accept of an invitation from the Seniors, before that of young men ; and refuſe nothing that is offered or ſet afore you : for they are very jealous, and ſenſible of the leaſt ſlighting or neglect from ſtrangers, and mindful of Revenge.

Touching TRADE with Indians.

IF you barely deſigne a Home-trade with neighbour-Indians, for skins of Deer, Beaver, Otter, Wild-Car, Fox, Racoon, &c. your beſt Truck is a ſort of courſe Trading Cloth, of which a yard and a half makes a Matchcoat or Mantle fit for their wear ; as alſo Axes, Hoes, Knives, Siſzars, and all ſorts of edg'd tools. Guns, Powder and Shot, &c. are Commodities they will greedily barter for : but to ſupply the Indians with Arms and Ammunition, is prohibited in all Engliſh Governments.

In dealing with the Indians, you muſt be poſitive and at a word : for if they perſwade you to fall any thing in your price, they will ſpend time in higgling for further abatements, and ſeldom conclude any Bargain. Sometimes you
may

may with Brandy or Strong liquor difpofe them to an hu-
mour of giving you ten times the value of your commodi-
ty ; and at other times they are fo hide-bound, that they
will not offer half the Market-price, efpecially if they be a-
ware that you have a defigne to circumvent them with drink,
or that they think you have a defire to their goods ; which
you muft feem to flight and difparage.

To the remoter Indians you muft carry other kinde of
Truck, as fmall Looking-glaffes, Pictures, Beads and Brace-
lets of glafs, Knives, Sizars, and all manner of gaudy toys
and knacks for children, which are light and portable. For
they are apt to admire fuch trinkets, and will purchafe them
at any rate, either with their currant Coyn of fmall fhells,
which they call *Roanoack* or *Peack*, or perhaps with Pearl,
Vermilion, pieces of Chriftal ; and towards *Ufhery*, with
fome odde pieces of Plate or Buillon, which they fometimes
receive in Truck from the *Oeftacks*.

Could I have forefeen when I fet out, the advantages to
be made by a Trade with thofe remote Indians, I had gone
better provided ; though perhaps I might have run a great
hazard of my life, had I purchafed confiderably amongft
them, by carrying wealth unguarded through fo many different Nations of barbarous people : therefore it is vain for
any man to propofe to himfelf, or undertake a Trade at that
diftance, unlefs he goes with ftrength to defend, as well as
an Adventure to purchafe fuch Commodities : for in fuch a
defigne many ought to joyn and go in company.

Some pieces of Silver unwrought I purchafed my felf of
the *Ufheries*, for no other end then to juftifie this account I
give of my Second Expedition, which had not determined
at *Ufhery*, were I accompanied with half a fcore refolute
youths that would have ftuck to me in a further difcovery
towards the Spanifh Mines.

F I N I S.